ITALIAN

Made Nice & Easy!®

Staff of Research & Education Association
Carl Fuchs, Language Program Director

Based on Language Courses developed by the
U.S. Government for Foreign Service Personnel

Research & Education Association
61 Ethel Road West
Piscataway, New Jersey 08854

Dr. M. Fogiel, Director

ITALIAN MADE NICE & EASY®

Year 2004 Printing

Copyright © 2001 by Research & Education Association. This copyright does not apply to the information included from U.S. Government publications which was edited by Research & Education Association.

Printed in the United States of America

Library of Congress Control Number 00-193027

International Standard Book Number 0-87891-371-8

What This Guide Will Do For You

Whether travelling to a foreign country or to your favorite international restaurant, this *Nice & Easy* guide gives you just enough of the language to get around and be understood. Much of the material in this book was developed for government personnel who are often assigned to a foreign country on a moment's notice and need a quick introduction to the language.

In this handy and compact guide, you will find useful words and phrases, popular expressions, common greetings, and the words for numbers, money, and time. Every word or phrase is accompanied with the correct pronunciation and spelling. There is a vocabulary list for finding words quickly.

Generous margins on the pages allow you to make notes and remarks that you may find helpful.

If you expect to travel to Italy, the section on the country's history and relevant up-to-date facts will make your trip more informative and enjoyable. By keeping this guide with you, you'll be well prepared to understand as well as converse in Italian.

Carl Fuchs
Language Program Director

Contents

Italian Facts and History v

Hints on Pronunciation 3

Useful Words and Phrases 5

Greetings and General Phrases 5

Location 6

Directions 7

Numbers 8

What's This 10

Asking For Things 10

Money 13

Time 13

Useful Phrases 15

Additions and Notes 16

Additional Expressions 17

Fill-In Sentences 19

Important Signs 31

Vocabulary List 35

ITALY

FACTS & HISTORY

Official Name: Republic of Italy

Geography
Area: 301,225 sq. km. (116,303 sq. mi.); about the size of Georgia and Florida combined.
Cities: *Capital*—Rome (pop. 2.7 million). *Other cities*—Milan, Naples, Turin.
Terrain: Mostly rugged and mountainous.
Climate: Generally mild Mediterranean; cold northern winters.

People
Nationality: *Noun and adjective*—Italian(s).
Population: 56.9 million.

Annual growth rate: 0.2%.

Ethnic groups: Primarily Italian, but there are small groups of German-, French-, Slovene-, and Albanian-Italians.

Religion: Roman Catholic (majority).

Language: Italian (official).

Education: *Years compulsory*—14. *Literacy*—98%.

Health: *Infant mortality rate*—8/1,000 live births. *Life expectancy*—74 yrs.

Work force (23 million): *Services*—61%.

History of Italy

Italy is largely homogeneous linguistically and religiously but is diverse culturally, economically, and politically. Italy has the fifth highest population density in Europe—about 200 persons per square kilometer. Minority groups are small, the two largest being the German-speaking people of Bolzano Province and the Slovenes around Trieste. Other groups comprise small communities of Albanian, Greek, Ladino, and French origin. Although Roman Catholicism is the majority religion—99% of the people are nominally Catholic—all religious faiths are provided equal freedom before the law by the constitution.

Greeks settled in the southern tip of the Italian Peninsula in the eighth and seventh centuries B.C.; Etruscans, Romans, and others inhabited the central and northern mainland. The peninsula subsequently was unified under the Roman Republic. The neighboring islands also came under Roman control by the third century B.C. By the first century A.D., the Roman Empire effectively dominated the Mediterranean world. After the collapse of the Roman Empire in the west in the fifth century A.D., the peninsula and islands were subjected to a series of invasions, and political unity was lost. Italy became an oft-changing succession of small states, principalities, and kingdoms which fought among themselves and were subject to ambitions of foreign powers. Popes of Rome ruled central Italy; rivalries between the popes and the Holy Roman Emperors, who claimed Italy as their domain, often made the peninsula a battleground.

The commercial prosperity of northern and central Italian cities, beginning in the 11th century, and the influence of the Renaissance mitigated somewhat the effects of these medieval political rivalries. Although Italy declined after the 16th century, the Renaissance had strengthened the idea of a single Italian nationality. By the early 19th century, a nationalist movement developed and led to the reunification of Italy—except for Rome—in the 1860s. In 1861, Victor Emmanuel II of the House of Savoy was proclaimed King of Italy. Rome was incorporated in 1870. From 1870 until 1922, Italy was a constitutional monarchy with a parliament elected under limited suffrage.

During World War I, Italy renounced its standing alliance with Germany and Austria-Hungary and, in 1915, entered the war on the side of the Allies. Under the postwar settlement, Italy received some former Austrian territory along the northeast frontier. In 1922, Benito Mussolini came to power and, over the next few years, eliminated political parties, curtailed personal liberties, and installed a fascist dictatorship termed the Corporate State. The king, with little or no effective power, remained titular head of state.

Italy then allied with Germany and declared war

on the United Kingdom and France in 1940. In 1941, Italy—with the other Axis powers, Germany and Japan—declared war on the United States and the Soviet Union. Following the Allied invasion of Sicily in 1943, the King dismissed Mussolini and appointed Marshal Pietro Badoglio as premier. The Badoglio government declared war on Germany, which quickly occupied most of the country and freed Mussolini, who led a brief-lived regime in the north. An antifascist popular resistance movement grew during the last two years of the war, harassing German forces before they were driven out in April 1945. The monarchy was ended by a 1946 plebiscite, and a constituent assembly was elected to draw up plans for the republic.

Under the 1947 peace treaty, minor adjustments were made in Italy's frontier with France. The eastern border area was transferred to Yugoslavia, and the area around the city of Trieste was designated a free territory. In 1954, the free territory, which had remained under the administration of U.S.-U.K. forces (Zone A, including the city of Trieste) and Yugoslav forces (Zone B), was divided between Italy and Yugoslavia, principally along the zonal boundary. This arrangement was made permanent by the Italian-Yugoslav

Treaty of Osimo, ratified in 1977. Under the 1947 peace treaty, Italy also gave up its overseas territories and certain Mediterranean islands.

The Roman Catholic Church's status in Italy has been determined, since its temporal powers ended in 1870, by a series of accords with the Italian government. Under the Lateran Pacts of 1929, which were confirmed by the present constitution, the state of Vatican City is recognized by Italy as an independent, sovereign entity. While preserving that recognition, in 1984, Italy and the Vatican updated several provisions of the 1929 accords. Included was the end of Roman Catholicism as Italy's formal state religion.

Italy's Cultural Contributions

Europe's Renaissance period began in Italy during the 14th and 15th centuries. Literary achievements—such as the poetry of Petrarch, Tasso, and Ariosto and the prose of Boccaccio, Machiavelli, and Castiglione—exerted a tremendous and lasting influence on the subsequent development of Western civilization, as did the painting, sculpture, and architecture contributed by giants such as Leonardo da Vinci, Raphael, Botticelli, Fra Angelico, and Michelangelo.

The musical influence of Italian composers Monteverdi, Palestrina, and Vivaldi proved epochal; in the 19th century, Italian romantic opera flourished under composers Gioacchino Rossini, Giuseppe Verdi, and Giacomo Puccini. Contemporary Italian artists, writers, filmmakers, architects, composers, and designers contribute significantly to Western culture.

Government & Politics

Italy has been a democratic republic since June 2, 1946, when the monarchy was abolished by popular referendum. The constitution was promulgated on January 1, 1948.

The Italian state is highly centralized. The prefect of each of the provinces is appointed by and answerable to the central government. In addition to the provinces, the constitution provides for 20 regions with limited governing powers. Five regions—Sardinia, Sicily, Trentino-Alto Adige, Valle d'Aosta, and Friuli-Venezia Giulia—function with special autonomy statutes. The other 15 regions were established in 1970 and vote for regional "councils." The establishment of regional governments throughout Italy has brought some decentralization to the national governmental machinery.

The 1948 constitution established a bicameral Parliament (Chamber of Deputies and Senate), a separate judiciary, and an executive branch composed of a Council of Ministers (cabinet) which is headed by the president of the council (prime minister). The president of the republic is elected for seven years by the Parliament sitting jointly with a small number of regional delegates. The president nominates the prime minister, who chooses the other ministers.

Trevi fountain, Rome

Campania, Positano

Vittorio Emmanuel Monument, Rome

Hints on Pronunciation

You will find all the words and phrases written both in Italian spelling and in a simplified spelling which you read like English. Don't use the Italian spelling, the one given in parentheses, unless you have studied Italian before. *Read the simplified spelling as though it were English.* When you see the Italian word for "excuse me" spelled *SKOO-za*, give the *oo* the sound it has in the English words *too*, *boot*, etc. and not the sound it has in German or any other language you may happen to know.

Each letter or combination of letters is used for the sound it usually stands for in English and it *always* stands for that sound. Thus, *oo* is always pronounced as it is in *boo, too, boot, tooth, roost*, never as anything else. Say these words and then pronounce the vowel sound by itself. That is the sound you must use every time you see *oo* in the *Pronunciation* column. If you should use some other sound—for example, the sound of *oo* in *blood*—you might be misunderstood.

Syllables that are accented, that is, pronounced louder than others, are written in capital letters. In Italian unaccented syllables are not skipped over quickly, as they are in English. Hyphens are used to divide words into syllables in order to make them easier to pronounce. Curved lines (‿) are used to show sounds that are pronounced together without any break; for example, *beek-K‿YAY-ray* meaning "glass," *D‿YAY-chee* meaning "ten."

Special Points

AY	as in *may, say, play* but don't drawl it the way we do in English. Since it is not drawled it sounds almost like the *e* in *let*. Example: *do-VAY* meaning "where is?"
O *or* **OH**	as in *go, so, oh, note, joke* but don't drawl it the way we do in English. Since it is not drawled it sounds somewhat like the *aw* in *law*. Example: *NO* meaning "no."

Leaning Tower of Pisa

Casa de Fauna, Pompeii

Major Church of San Giorgia, Venice

GREETINGS AND GENERAL PHRASES

English	*Pronunciation and Italian Spelling*
Good morning *or* Good day	*bwohn JOR-no* (Buon giorno)
Good evening	*BWO-na SAY-ra* (Buona sera)
Sir *or* Mister	*seen-YO-ray* (signore)
Madam	*seen-YO-ra* (signora)
Miss	*seen-yo-REE-na* (signorina)

Italians have two phrases for "please" which they use very often. They are:

Please	*payr p̲ya-CHAY-ray* (per piacere)
or	*payr fa-VO-ray* (per favore)
Excuse me	*SKOO-za* (scusa)

English	Pronunciation and Italian Spelling
Thank you	*GRAHTS-yay* (grazie)
Yes	*SEE* (sì)
No	*NO* (no)
Do you understand?	*ah-VAY-tay ka-PEE-to?* (Avete capito?)
I don't understand	*NOHN ka-PEE-sko* (Non capisco)
Speak slowly	*par-LA-tay ah-DA-jo* (Parlate adagio)

LOCATION

When you need directions to get somewhere you use the phrase "where is" and then add the words you need.

Where is	*[DO-vay AY] do VAY* ([Dove è] Dov'è)
the restaurant?	*eel ress-to-RAHN* (il restaurant)
Where is the restaurant?	*[DO-vay AY] do-VAY eel ress-to-RAHN?* ([Dove è] Dov'è il restaurant?)
hotel	*o-TEL* (hotel)
or	*ahl-BAYR-go* (albergo)
Where is a hotel?	*[DO-vay AY] do-VAY lo-TEL?* ([Dove è] Dov'è l'hotel?)
or	*[DO-vay AY] do-VAY lahl-BAYR-go?* ([Dove è] Dov'è l'albergo?)
the railroad station	*la stahts-YO-nay* (la stazione)

English	Pronunciation and Italian Spelling
Where is the railroad station?	[*DO-vay A Y*] *do-VA Y la stahts-YO-nay?* ([Dove è] Dov'è la stazione?)
a toilet	*eel ga-bee-NET-to* il gabinetto
Where is a toilet?	[*DO-vay-A Y*] *do-VA Y eel ga-bee-NET-to?* ([Dove è] Dov'è il gabinetto?)

DIRECTIONS

The answer to your question "Where is such and such" may be "Turn right," or "Turn left" or "Straight ahead," so you need to know these phrases:

Turn right	*JEE-ra ah DESS-tra*	(Gira a destra)
Turn left	*JEE-ra ah see-NEE-stra*	(Gira a sinistra)
Straight ahead	*SEM-pray dee-REET-to*	(Sempre diritto)

Paestum

7

It is sometimes useful to say "Please point."

Please point   *een-dee-KA-tay-mee, payr fa-VO-ray*
                              (Indicatemi, per favore)

If you are driving and ask the distance to another town it will be given to you in kilometers, not miles.

Kilometers   *kee-LO-may-tree*   chilometri

One kilometer equals ⅝ of a mile.

NUMBERS

You need to know the numbers.

English	Pronunciation	Italian
One	*OO-no*	uno
Two	*DOO-ay*	due
Three	*TRAY*	tre
Four	*KWAHT-tro*	quattro
Five	*CHEEN-kway*	cinque
Six	*SAY*	sei
Seven	*SET-tay*	sette
Eight	*OHT-to*	otto
Nine	*NO-vay*	nove
Ten	*D‿YAY-chee*	dieci
Eleven	*OON-dee-chee*	undici

English	Pronunciation and Italian Spelling	
Twelve	*DO-dee-chee*	dodici
Thirteen	*TRAY-dee-chee*	tredici
Fourteen	*kwaht-TOR-dee-chee*	quattordici
Fifteen	*KWEEN-dee-chee*	quindici
Sixteen	*SAY-dee-chee*	sedici
Seventeen	*dee-chahss-SET-tay*	diciassette
Eighteen	*dee-CHOHT-to*	diciotto
Nineteen	*dee-chahn-NO-vay*	diciannove
Twenty	*VEN-tee*	venti
Twenty-one	*ven-TOO-no*	ventuno
Twenty-two	*ven-tee-DOO-ay*	ventidue (and so forth)
Thirty	*TREN-ta*	trenta
Thirty-one	*tren-TOO-no*	trentuno
Thirty-two	*tren-ta-DOO-ay*	trentadue (and so forth)
Forty	*kwa-RAHN-ta*	quaranta
Fifty	*cheen-KWAHN-ta*	cinquanta
Sixty	*sess-SAHN-ta*	sessanta
Seventy	*set-TAHN-ta*	settanta

English	Pronunciation and Italian Spelling	
Eighty	*oht-TAHN-ta*	ottanta
Ninety	*no-VAHN-ta*	novanta
Hundred	*CHEN-to*	cento
Thousand	*MEEL-lay*	mille

WHAT'S THIS?

When you want to know the name of something you can say "What's this?" and point to the thing you mean.

What is	[*KO-za AY*] *ko-ZAY* ([Cosa è] Cos'è)
this	*KWESS-to* (questo)
What's this?	[*KO-za AY*] *ko-ZAY KWESS-to?* ([Cosa è] Cos'è questo?)

ASKING FOR THINGS

When you want something, you can say "I want" and add the name of the thing wanted.

I want	*EE⌣o day-ZEE-day-ro* (Io desidero)
or	*EE⌣o VOHL-yo* (Io voglio)
cigarettes	*see-ga-RET-tay* (sigarette)
I want cigarettes	*EE⌣o day-ZEE-day-ro see-ga-RET-tay* (Io desidero sigarette)
to eat	*mahn-JA-ray* (mangiare)
I want to eat	*EE⌣o day-ZEE-day-ro mahn-JA-ray* (Io desidero mangiare)

10

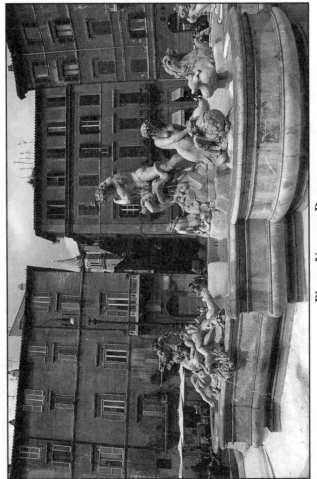

Piazza Navona, Rome

Santa Maria Del Fiore Cathedral, Florence

English	Pronunciation and Italian Spelling

Here are the words for some of the things you may require:

bread	*PA-nay* (pane)
butter	*BOOR-ro* (burro)
soup	*mee-NESS-tra* (minestra)
fish	*PAY-shay* (pesce)
meat	*KAR-nay* (carne)
steak	*bee-STEK-ka* (bistecca)
lamb	*ahn-YEL-lo* (agnello)
veal	*vee-TEL-lo* (vitello)
pork	*ma-YA-lay* (maiale)
beef	*MAHN-dzo* (manzo)
chicken	*POHL-lo* (pollo)
eggs	*WO-va* (uova)
fruit	*FROOT-ta* (frutta)
vegetables	*vayr-DOO-ra* (verdura)
or	*lay-GOO-mee* (legumi)
potatoes	*pa-TA-tay* (patate)
beans	*fa-JO-lee* (fagioli)
sugar	*TSOOK-kay-ro* (zucchero)

English	Pronunciation and Italian Spelling
salt	*SA-lay* (sale)
pepper	*PAY-pay* (pepe)
rice	*REE-zo* (riso)
salad	*een-sa-LA-ta* (insalata)
tomato	*po-mo-DO-ro* (pomodoro)
orange	*ah-RAHN-cha* (arancia)
lemon	*lee-MO-nay* (limone)
milk	*LAHT-tay* (latte)
ice cream	*jay-LA-to* (gelato)
chocolate	*chohk-ko-LA-ta* (cioccolata)
tobacco	*ta-BAHK-ko* (tabacco)
drinking water	*AHK-kwa po-TA-bee-lay* (acqua potabile)
cup of tea	*TAHT-tsa dee TAY* (tazza di tè)
cup of coffee	*TAHT-tsa dee kahf-FAY* (tazza di caffè)
glass of beer	*beek-K⌣YAY-ray dee BEER-ra* (bicchiere di birra)
bottle of wine	*F⌣YA-sko dee VEE-no* (fiasco di vino)
matches	*f⌣yahm-MEE-fay-ree* (fiammiferi)

MONEY

To find out how much things cost you say "How much costs?"

How much	*KWAHN-to*	Quanto
costs	*KO-sta*	costa
How much does this cost?	*KWAHN-to KO-sta?*	Quanto costa?

TIME

To find out what time it is you say "What hour is it?"

What time is it? *kay O-ra AY?* (Che ora è?)

For "Two o'clock" you say "They are the two."

Two o'clock *SO-no lay DOO-ay* (sono le due)

"Ten past two" is "The two and ten."

Ten past two *lay DOO-ay ay D⌣YAY-chee*
(le due e dieci)

"Quarter past five" is "The five and a quarter."

Quarter past five *lay CHEEN-kway ay oon KWAHR-to*
(le cinque e un quarto)

"Half past six" is "The six and a half."

Half past six *lay SAY ay MED-dza* (le sei e mezza)

13

English	Pronunciation and Italian Spelling

"Quarter of eight" is "The eight minus a quarter."

Quarter of eight   *lay OHT-to MAY-no oon KWAR-to*
(le otto meno un quarto)

You may also say:

oon KWAR-to AHL-lay OHT-to
(un quarto alle otto)

"Three minutes to nine" is "The nine minus three."

Three minutes to nine   *lay NO-vay MAY-no TRAY*
(le nove meno tre)

If you want to know when a movie starts or when the train leaves you say:

At what hour   *ah KAY O-ra*   (A che ora)

begins   *ko-MEEN-cha*   (comincia)

the film   *eel FEELM*   (il film)

When does the movie start?   *ah KAY O-ra ko-MEEN-cha eel FEELM?*
(A che ora comincia il film?)

the train   *eel TRAY-no*   (il treno)

leaves   *PAR-tay*   (parte)

When does the train leave?   *ah KAY O-ra PAR-tay eel TRAY-no?*
(A che ora parte il treno?)

Yesterday   *YAY-ree*   (ieri)

English	Pronunciation and Italian Spelling
Today	*OHD-jee* (oggi)
Tomorrow	*do-MA-nee* (domani)

The days of the week are:

Sunday	*do-MAY-nee-ka* (domenica)
Monday	*loo-nay-DEE* (lunedì)
Tuesday	*mar-tay-DEE* (martedì)
Wednesday	*mayr-ko-lay-DEE* (mercoledì)
Thursday	*jo-vay-DEE* (giovedì)
Friday	*vay-nayr-DEE* (venerdì)
Saturday	*SA-ba-to* (sabato)

USEFUL PHRASES

The following phrases will be useful:

What is your name?	*KO-may see K‿YA-ma?* (Come si chiama?)
My name is___	*EE‿o mee K‿YA-mo___* (Io mi chiamo___)
How do you say *table* (or anything else) in Italian?	*KO-may see K‿YA-ma* table *een ee-tahl-YA-no?* (Come si chiama *table* in italiano?)
Good-by	*ar-ree-vay-DAYR-chee* (Arrivederci)

ADDITIONS AND NOTES

Another way to say restaurant is:

eel ree-sto-RAHN-tay   (il ristorante)

A *F⌣YA-sko* is a bottle containing 2 liters, equal to about half a gallon. In Italy wine is generally sold in bottles of this size.

Another common way to say the sentence "How do you say *table* in Italian?" is:

KO-may see DEE-chay table *een ee-tahl-YA-no?*   (Come si dice *table* in italiano?)

Montepulciano

Castle of Cornedo

Vallombrosa, Tuscany

Gondola tour, Venice

ADDITIONAL EXPRESSIONS

English	Pronunciation and Italian Spelling
I am hungry	*O FA-may* (Ho fame)
I am thirsty	*O SAY-tay* (Ho sete)
I am well	*STO BAY-nay* (Sto bene)
Stop!	*fayr-MA-tay-vee!* (Fermatevi!)
Come here!	*vay-NEE-tay KWEE!* (Venite quì!)
Right away *or* Quickly	*PRESS-to* (Presto)
Come quickly!	*vay-NEE-tay PRESS-to!* (Venite presto!)
Go quickly!	*ahn-DA-tay PRESS-to!* (Andate presto!)
Help!	*ah-YOO-to!* (Aiuto!)
Help me	*ah-yoo-TA-tay-mee* (Aiutatemi)
Bring help	*k⏜ya-MA-tay day sohk-KOR-see* (Chiamate dei soccorsi)
I will pay you	*VEE pa-gay-RO* (Vi pagherò)
Where is the town?	*do-VAY eel pa-AY-zay?* (Dov'è il paese?)

English	Pronunciation and Italian Spelling
Where is it?	*do-VAY?* (Dov'è?)
How far is the town?	*ah KAY deess-TAHN-tsa AY eel pa-AY-zay?* (A che distanza è il paese?)
Is it far?	*AY lohn-TA-no?* (È lontano?)
How far is it?	*ah KAY dee-STAHN-tsa AY?* (A che distanza è?)
Which way is north?	*do-VAY eel NORD?* (Dov'è il nord?)
Which is the road to___?	*kwa-LAY la STRA-da payr___?* (Qual'è la strada per___?)
Draw me a map	*FA-tay-mee oo-no SKEET-tso* (Fatemi uno schizzo)
Take me there	*ahk-kohm-pahn-YA-tay-mee LA* (Accompagnatemi là)
Take me to a doctor	*ahk-kohm-pahn-YA-tay-mee da oon MAY-dee-ko* (Accompagnatemi da un medico)
Take me to the hospital	*ahk-kohm-pahn-YA-tay-mee ahl-lo-spay-DA-lay* (Accompagnatemi all'ospedale)
Danger!	*pay-REE-ko-lo!* (Pericolo!)
Watch out!	*aht-tents-YO-nay!* (Attenzione!)
Gas!	*GAHSS!* (Gas!)
Take cover!	*MET-tayr-see ahl ree-PA-ro!* (Mettersi al riparo!)
Wait a minute!	*ah-spet-TA-tay oon mee-NOO-to!* (Aspettate un minuto!)
Good luck	*BWO-na for-TOO-na* (Buona fortuna)

Park D'Alassio Fountain, Riviera

Duomo Cathedral, Milan

FILL-IN SENTENCES

In this section you will find a number of sentences, each containing a blank space which can be filled in with any one of the words in the list that follows. For example, in order to say "Where can I get some soap?" look for the phrase "Where can I get___?" in the English column and find the Italian expression given beside it; in this case it is *DO-vay POHSS-so tro-VA-ray___*. Then look for "soap" in the list that follows; the Italian is *del sa-PO-nay*. Put the word for "soap" in the blank space and you get *DO-vay POHSS-so tro-VA-ray del sa-PO-nay?*

English	*Pronunciation and Italian Spelling*
I want___	*day-ZEE-day-ro___* (Desidero___)
We want___	*day-zee-dayr-YA-mo___* (Desideriamo___)
Give me___	*DA-tay-mee___* (Datemi___)
Bring me___	*por-TA-tay-mee___* (Portatemi___)
Where can I get___?	*DO-vay POHSS-so tro-VA-ray___?* (Dove posso trovare___?)
I have___	*O___* (Ho___)
We have___	*ahb-B⌣YA-mo___* (Abbiamo___)
I don't have___	*nohn O___* (Non ho___)
We don't have___	*nohn ahb-B⌣YA-mo___* (Non abbiamo___)
Have you___?	*ah-VAY-tay___?* (Avete___?)

English	Pronunciation and Italian Spelling
	EXAMPLE
I want___	*day-ZEE-day-ro___* (Desidero___)
food	*da mahn-JA-ray* (da mangiare)
I want food	*day-ZEE-day-ro da mahn-JA-ray*
	(Desidero da mangiare)

food	*da mahn-JA-ray* (da mangiare)
apples	*MAY-lay* (mele)
boiled water	*del-LAHK-kwa bohl-LEE-ta* (dell'acqua bollita)
carrots	*ka-RO-tay* (carote)
cucumbers	*chee-tree-O-lee* (citrioli)
grapes	*OO-va* (uva)
ham	*pro-SHOOT-to* (prosciutto)
onions	*chee-POHL-lay* (cipolle)
peas	*pee-ZEL-lee* (piselli)
spinach	*spee-NA-chee* (spinaci)
turnips	*RA-pay* (rape)
(*for other foods see page 10*)	
a cup	*oo-na TAHT-tsa* (una tazza)
a fork	*oo-na for-KET-ta* (una forchetta)

English	Pronunciation and Italian Spelling
a glass	*oon beek-K_YAY-ray* (un bicchiere)
a knife	*oon kohl-TEL-lo* (un coltello)
a plate	*oon P_YAHT-to* (un piatto)
a spoon	*oon kook-K_YA-yo* (un cucchiaio)
a bed	*oon LET-to* (un letto)
blankets	*del-lay ko-PAYR-tay* (delle coperte)
a mattress	*oon ma-tay-RAHSS-so* (un materasso)
a pillow	*oon koo-SHEE-no* (un cuscino)
a room	*oo-na KA-may-ra* (una camera)
sheets	*del-lay lent-SWO-la* (delle lenzuola)
a towel	*oon ah-shoo-ga-MA-no* (un'asciugamano)
cigars	*DAY SEE-ga-ree* (dei sigari)
a pipe	*oo-na PEE-pa* (una pipa)
tobacco	*del ta-BAHK-ko* (del tabacco)
pipe tobacco	*ta-BAHK-ko payr PEE-pa* (tabacco per pipa)
a pen	*oo-na PEN-na* (una penna)
a pencil	*oo-na ma-TEE-ta* (una matita)
ink	*del-leenk-YOHS-tro* (dell'inchiostro)

21

English	Pronunciation and Italian Spelling
a comb	*oon PET-tee-nay* (un pettine)
hot water	*del-LAHK-kwa KAHL-da* (dell'acqua calda)
a razor	*oon ra-ZO-yo* (un rasoio)
razor blades	*del-lay LA-may da ra-ZO-yo* (delle lame da rasoio)
a shaving brush	*oon pen-NEL-lo payr BAR-ba* (un pennello per barba)
shaving soap	*del sa-PO-nay payr BAR-ba* (del sapone per barba)
soap	*del sa-PO-nay* (del sapone)
a tooth-brush	*oo-no spat-tso-LEE-no da DEN-tee* (uno spazzolino da denti)
tooth paste	*del-la PA-sta den-tee-FREE-cha* (della pasta dentifricia)
tooth powder	*pohl-VAY-ray den-tee-FREE-cha* (polvere dentifricia)
a handker-chief	*oon faht-tso-LET-to* (un fazzoletto)
a raincoat	*oon eem-payr-may-AH-bee-lay* (un impermeabile)
a shirt	*oo-na ka-MEE-cha* (una camicia)

22

English	Pronunciation and Italian Spelling
shoe laces	*day LAHT-chee da SKAR-pay* (dei lacci da scarpe)
shoe polish	*del-la CHAY-ra payr SKAR-pay* (della cera per scarpe)
shoes	*del-lay SKAR-pay* (delle scarpe)
undershirt	*oo-na MAHL-ya* (una maglia)
under-shorts	*del-lay moo-TAHN-day* (delle mutande)
a needle	*oon AH-go* (un ago)
buttons	*day boht-TO-nee* (dei bottoni)
safety pins	*dayl-yee SPEEL-lee dee see-koo-RET-tsa* (degli spilli di sicurezza)
thread	*del FEE-lo da koo-CHEE-ray* (del filo da cucire)
adhesive tape	*chay-ROHT-to* (cerotto)
aspirin	*del-la-spee-REE-na* (dell'aspirina)
a bandage	*oo-na BEN-da* (una benda)
cotton	*del ko-TO-nay* (del cotone)
a disin-fectant	*oon dee-zeen-fet-TAHN-tay* (un disinfettante)
iodine	*teen-TOO-ra DOHD-yo* (tintura d'odio)
a laxative	*oon lahss-sa-TEE-vo* (un lassativo)

23

English	Pronunciation and Italian Spelling
	EXAMPLE
I want to___	*day-ZEE-day-ro___* (Desidero___)
eat	*mahn-JA-ray* (mangiare)
I want to eat	*day-ZEE-day-ro mahn-JA-ray* (Desidero mangiare)
eat	*mahn-JA-ray* (mangiare)
drink	*BAY-ray* (bere)
wash up	*la-VAR-mee* (lavarmi)
take a bath	*PREN-day-ray oon BAHN-yo* (prendere un bagno)
rest	*ree-po-ZA-ray* (riposare)
sleep	*dor-MEE-ray* (dormire)
have my hair cut	*FAR-mee tahl-YA-ray ee ka-PEL-lee* (farmi tagliare i capelli)
be shaved	*FAR-mee la BAR-ba* (farmi la barba)
have my clothes washed	*FAR la-VA-ray DEL-la b_yahn-kay-REE-ah* (far lavare della biancheria)

A simple way of asking for a haircut in Italian is to use the word for "hair," which is *ka-PEL-lee*. When you want a shave, you can use the word for "beard," *BAR-ba*.

English	Pronunciation and Italian Spelling
Where is there___?	*DO-vay CHAY___?* (Dove c'è___?)
Where can I find___?	*DO-vay POHSS-so tro-VA-ray___?* (Dove posso trovare___?)

EXAMPLE

Where is there___?	*DO-vay CHAY___?* (Dove c'è___?)
a barber	*oon barb-YAY-ray* (un barbiere)
Where is there a barber?	*DO-vay CHAY oon barb-YAY-ray?* (Dove c'è un barbiere?)

a barber	*oon barb-YAY-ray* (un barbiere)
a dentist	*oon den-TEE-sta* (un dentista)
a doctor	*oon MAY-dee-ko* (un medico)
a mechanic	*oon mek-KA-nee-ko* (un meccanico)
a policeman	*oo-na GWARD-ya* (una guardia)
a porter	*oon fahk-KEE-no* (un facchino)
a servant	*oon ka-mayr-YAY-ray* (un cameriere)
a shoe-maker	*oon kahl-tso-LA-yo* (un calzolaio)
a tailor	*oon SAR-to* (un sarto)
a workman	*oon o-pay-RA-yo* (un operaio)

25

English	Pronunciation and Italian Spelling
a church	*oo-na K⌣YAY-za* (una chiesa)
a clothing store	*oon nay-GOHTS-yo dee ar-TEE-ko-lee da WO-mo* (un negozio di articoli da uomo)
a drugstore	*oo-na far-ma-CHEE-ah* (una farmacia)
a garage	*oon ga-RAJ* (un garage)
a grocery	*oon nay-GOHTS-yo dee JAY-nay-ree ah-lee-men-TA-ree* (un negozio di generi alimentari)
a house	*oo-na KA-za* (una casa)
a spring	*oo-na sor-JEN-tay* (una sorgente)
a well	*oon POHT-tso* (un pozzo)

Where is___?	*do-VAY___?* (Dov'è___?)

EXAMPLE

Where is___?	*do-VAY___?* (Dov'è___?)
the bridge	*eel POHN-tay* (il ponte)
Where is the bridge?	*do-VAY eel POHN-tay?* (Dov'è il ponte?)

the bridge	*eel POHN-tay* (il ponte)
the bus	*LA⌣oo-to-booss* (l'autobus)

English	Pronunciation and Italian Spelling
the camp	*eel KAHM-po* (il campo)
the city	*la cheet-TA* (la città)
the highway	*la␣oo-to-STRA-da* (l'autostrada)
the hospital	*lo-spay-DA-lay* (l'ospedale)
the main street	*la STRA-da preen-chee-PA-lay* (la strada principale)
the market	*eel mayr-KA-to* (il mercato)
the nearest town	*eel pa-AY-zay P␣YOO vee-CHEE-no* (il paese più vicino)
the police station	*la kwess-TOO-ra* (la questura)
the post office	*loof-FEE-cho po-STA-lay* (l'ufficio postale)
the railroad	*la fayr-ro-VEE-ah* (la ferrovia)
the river	*eel F␣YOO-may* (il fiume)
the road	*la STRA-da* (la strada)
the telegraph office	*loof-FEE-cho tay-lay-GRA-fee-ko* (l'ufficio telegrafico)
the telephone	*eel tay-LAY-fo-no* (il telefono)
the town	*eel pa-AY-zay* (il paese)

English	Pronunciation and Italian Spelling
I am___	*SO-no___* (Sono___)
He is___	*EL-yee A Y___* (Egli è___)

EXAMPLE

I am___	*SO-no___* (Sono___)
an American	*ah-may-ree-KA-no* (americano)
I am an American	*SO-no ah-may-ree-KA-no* (Sono americano)
an American	*ah-may-ree-KA-no* (americano)
sick	*ahm-ma-LA-to* (ammalato)
wounded	*fay-REE-to* (ferito)
lost	*spayr-DOO-to* (sperduto)
tired	*STAHN-ko* (stanco)

We are___	*S⌣YA-mo___* (Siamo___)
They are___	*ESS-see SO-no___* (Essi sono___)
Are you___?	*S⌣YA Y-tay___?* (Siete___?)

EXAMPLE

We are___	*S⌣YA-mo___* (Siamo___)
Americans	*ah-may-ree-KA-nee* (americani)
We are Americans	*S⌣YA-mo ah-may-ree-KA-nee* (Siamo americani)

Scaliger's Castle. Sirmione

English	Pronunciation and Italian Spelling
Americans	*ah-may-ree-KA-nee* (americani)
sick	*ahm-ma-LA-tee* (ammalati)
wounded	*fay-REE-tee* (feriti)
lost	*spayr-DOO-tee* (sperduti)
tired	*STAHN-kee* (stanchi)

It is___	*A Y___* (È___)
Is it___?	*A Y___?* (È___?)
It is not___	*nohn A Y___* (Non è___)

29

English	Pronunciation and Italian Spelling
	EXAMPLE
It is not___	*nohn AY___* (Non è___)
good	*BWO-no* (buono)
It is not good	*nohn AY BWO-no* (Non è buono)
good	*BWO-no* (buono)
bad	*kaht-TEE-vo* (cattivo)
expensive	*KA-ro* (caro)
too expen-sive	*TROHP-po KA-ro* (troppo caro)
here	*KWEE* (quì)
there	*LA* (là)
near	*vee-CHEE-no* (vicino)
far	*lohn-TA-no* (lontano)

30

IMPORTANT SIGNS

Italian	English
Alt!	Stop!
Rallentare!	Go Slow!
Pericolo!	Danger!
Senso unico	One Way
Senso vietato	No Thoroughfare
Tenere la destra	Keep to the Right
Strada in costruzione	Road under Construction
Curva pericolosa	Dangerous Curve
A 300 metri arresto	Stop at 300 Meters
Attenti ai treni	Look Out for Locomotive
Pericolo di morte	High Tension Lines (Danger of death)
Incrocio pericoloso	Dangerous Crossing
Passaggio a livello	Grade Crossing
Divieto di parcheggio	No Parking
Vietato l'ingresso	No Admittance
Donne or Signore	Women
Uomini or Signori	Men
Vietato fumare	No Smoking
Vietato sputare	No Spitting
Entrata	Entrance
Uscita	Exit

Mantua, Lombardy

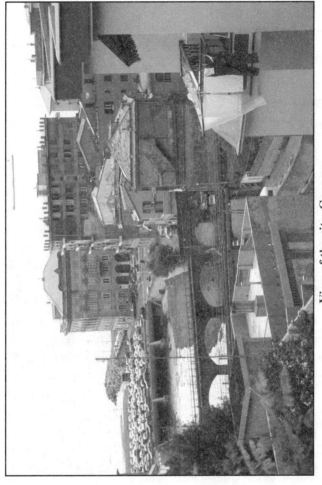

View of the city, Genoa

Colosseum, Rome

Old fortifications, Umbria, Assisi

Siena

ALPHABETICAL
WORD LIST

English	Pronunciation and Italian Spelling

A

a	*oon* (un)
or	*oo-na* (una)
adhesive tape	*chay-ROHT-to* (cerotto)
am	
I am	*SO-no* (sono)
American	*ah-may-ree-KA-no* (americano)
Americans	*ah-may-ree-KA-nee* (americani)
and	*ay* (e)
apples	*MAY-lay* (mele)
are	
Are you?	*S͜YAY-tay?* (Siete?)
They are	*ESS-see SO-no* (Essi sono)
We are	*S͜YA-mo* (Siamo)
aspirin	*ah-spee-REE-na* (aspirina)

35

English	Pronunciation and Italian Spelling

B

bad	*kaht-TEE-vo* (cattivo)
bandage	*BEN-da* (benda)
barber	*barb-YAY-ray* (barbiere)
be shaved	
I want to be shaved	*day-ZEE-day-ro FAR-mee la BAR-ba* (Desidero farmi la barba)
beans	*fa-JO-lee* (fagioli)
bed	*LET-to* (letto)
beef	*MAHN-dzo* (manzo)
beer	*BEER-ra* (birra)
a glass of beer	*oon beek-K͜YAY-ray dee BEER-ra* (un bicchiere di birra)
blankets	*ko-PAYR-tay* (coperte)
boiled water	*AK-kwa bohl-LEE-ta* (acqua bollita)
bottle	*F͜YA-sko* (fiasco)
a bottle of	*oon F͜YA-sko dee___* (un fiasco di__)
bread	*PA-nay* (pane)
bridge	*POHN-tay* (ponte)
bring help	*k͜ya-MA-tay day sohk-KOR-see* (Chiamate dei soccorsi)

English	Pronunciation and Italian Spelling
Bring me___	*por-TA-tay-mee___* (Portatemi___)
brush	
shaving brush	*pen-NEL-lo payr BAR-ba* (pennello per barba)
bus	*A͜oo-to-booss* (autobus)
butter	*BOOR-ro* (burro)
buttons	*boht-TO-nee* (bottoni)

C

camp	*KAHM-po* (campo)
can	
I can	*POHSS-so* (Posso)
carrots	*ka-RO-tay* (carote)
centesimi	*chen-TAY-zee-mee* (centesimi)
chicken	*POHL-lo* (pollo)
chocolate	*chohk-ko-LA-ta* (cioccolata)
church	*K͜YAY-za* (chiesa)
cigarettes	*see-ga-RET-tay* (sigarette)
cigars	*SEE-ga-ree* (sigari)
city	*cheet-TA* (città)

37

English	Pronunciation and Italian Spelling
clothing store	*nay-GOHTS-yo dee ar-TEE-ko-lee da WO-mo* (negozio di articoli da uomo)
coffee	*kahf-FAY* (caffe)
a cup of coffee	*oo-na TAHT-tsa dee kahf-FAY* (una tazza di caffè)
comb	*PET-tee-nay* (pettine)
come	*vay-NEE-tay* (venite)
Come here	*vay-NEE-tay KWEE* (Venite qui)
Come quickly	*vay-NEE-tay PRESS-to* (Venite presto)
cost	
it costs	*KO-sta* (costa)
How much does this cost?	*KWAHN-to KO-sta?* (Quanto costa?)
cotton	*ko-TO-nay* (cotone)
cover	
Take cover!	*MET-tayr-see ahl ree-PA-ro!* (Mettersi al riparo!)
cucumbers	*cheet-R⌣YO-lee* (citrioli)
cup	*TAHT-tsa* (tazza)
a cup of___	*oo-na TAHT-tsa dee___* (una tazza di___)

English	Pronunciation and Italian Spelling

D

Danger!	*pay-REE-ko-lo!* (Pericolo!)
day	*JOR-no* (giorno)
Good day	*bwohn JOR-no* (Buon giorno)
dentist	*den-TEE-sta* (dentista)
disinfectant	*dee-zeen-fet-TAHN-tay* (disinfettante)
Do you understand?	*ah-VAY-tay ka-PEE-to?* (Avete capito?)
doctor	*MAY-dee-ko* (medico)
Take me to a doctor	*ahk-kohm-pahn-YA-tay-mee da oon MAY-dee-ko* (Accompagnatemi da un medico)
Draw me a map	*FA-tay-mee oo-no SKEET-tso* (Fatemi uno schizzo)
drink	*BAY-ray* (bere)
drinking water	*AHK-kwa po-TA-bee-lay* (acqua potabile)
drugstore	*far-ma-CHEE-ah* (farmacia)

E

eat	*mahn-JA-ray* (mangiare)
eggs	*WO-va* (uova)
eight	*OHT-to* (otto)

39

English	Pronunciation and Italian Spelling
eighteen	*dee-CHOHT-to* (diciotto)
eighty	*oht-TAHN-ta* (ottanta)
eleven	*OON-dee-chee* (undici)
evening	*SAY-ra* (sera)
Good evening	*BWO-na SAY-ra* (Buona sera)
Excuse me	*SKOO-za* (scusa)
expensive	*KA-ro* (caro)
too expensive	*TROHP-po KA-ro* (troppo caro)

F

far	*lohn-TA-no* (lontano)
How far is it?	*ah KAY dee-STAHN-tsa AY?* (A che distanza è?)
Is it far?	*AY lohn-TA-no?* (È lontano?)
fifteen	*KWEEN-dee-chee* (quindici)
fifty	*cheen-KWAHN-ta* (cinquanta)
find	*tro-VA-ray* (trovare)
Where can I find___?	*DO-vay POHSS-so tro-VA-ray___?* (Dove posso trovare___?)
fish	*PAY-shay* (pesce)

English	Pronunciation and Italian Spelling
five	*CHEEN-kway* (cinque)
food	*da mahn-JA-ray* (da mangiare)
fork	*for-KET-ta* (forchetta)
forty	*kwa-RAHN-ta* (quaranta)
four	*KWAHT-tro* (quattro)
fourteen	*kwaht-TOR-dee-chee* (quattordici)
Friday	*vay-nayr-DEE* (venerdì)
fruit	*FROOT-ta* (frutta)

G

garage	*ga-RAJ* (garage)
Gas!	*GAHSS!* (Gas!)
get	
Where can I get___?	*DO-vay POHSS-so tro-VA-ray___?* (Dove posso trovare___?)
Give me___	*DA-tay-mee___* (Datemi___)
glass	*beek-K͜YAY-ray* (bicchiere)
a glass of___	*oon beek-K͜YAY-ray dee___* (un bicchiere di___)
go	*ahn-DA-tay!* (Andate!)
Go quickly	*ahn-DA-tay PRESS-to!* (Andate presto!)

41

English	Pronunciation and Italian Spelling
good	*BWO-no* (buono)
Good day	*bwohn JOR-no* (Buon giorno)
Good evening	*BWO-na SAY-ra* (Buona sera)
Good luck	*BWO-na for-TOO-na* (Buona fortuna)
Good morning	*bwohn JOR-no* (Buon giorno)
Good-by	*ar-ree-vay-DAYR-chee* (Arrivederci)
grapes	*OO-va* (uva)
grocery	*nay-GOHTS-yo dee JAY-nay-ree ah-lee-men-TA-ree* (negozio di generi alimentari)

H

hair	*ka-PEL-lee* (capelli)
have my hair cut	*FAR-mee tahl-YA-ray ee ka-PEL-lee* (farmi tagliare i capelli)
half	
half past six	*lay SAY ay MED-dza* (le sei e mezza)
Halt!	*AHL-to LA!* (Alto là!)
ham	*pro-SHOOT-to* (prosciutto)
handkerchief	*faht-tso-LET-to* (fazzoletto)

English	Pronunciation and Italian Spelling
have	
Have you?	*ah-VAY-tay?* (Avete?)
I have	*O* (Ho)
I don't have	*nohn O* (Non ho)
We have	*ahb-B⌣YA-mo* (Abbiamo)
We don't have	*nohn ahb-B⌣YA-mo* (Non abbiamo)
have my clothes washed	*FAR la-VA-ray del-la b⌣yahn-kay-REE-ah* (far lavare della biancheria)
have my hair cut	*FAR-mee tahl-YA-ray ee ka-PEL-lee* (farmi tagliare i capelli)
he	*EL-yee* (egli)
he is	*EL-yee AY* (Egli è)
Help!	*ah-YOO-to!* (Aiuto!)
Bring help	*k⌣ya-MA-tay day sohk-KOR-see* (Chiamate dei soccorsi)
Help me	*ah-yoo-TA-tay-mee* (Aiutatemi)
here	*KWEE* (quì)
highway	*a⌣oo-to-STRA-da* (autostrada)
hospital	*o-spay-DA-lay* (ospedale)
Take me to the hospital	*ahk-kohm-pahn-YA-tay-mee ahl-lo-spay-DA-lay* (Accompagnatemi all'ospedale)

English	Pronunciation and Italian Spelling
hot water	*AHK-kwa KAHL-da* (acqua calda)
hotel	*o-TEL* (hotel)
Where is a hotel?	*do-VAY lo-TEL?* (Dov'è l'hotel?)
house	*KA-za* (casa)
how	*KO-may* (come)
How do you say___?	*KO-may see K‿YA-ma___?* (Come si chiama___?)
or	*KO-may see DEE-chay___?* (Come si dice___?)
How far is it?	*ah KAY dee-STAHN-tsa AY?* (A che distanza è?)
How much	*KWAHN-to* (quanto)
How much does this cost?	*KWAHN-to KO-sta?* (Quanto costa?)
hundred	*CHEN-to* (cento)
hungry	
I am hungry	*O FA-may* (Ho fame)

I

I	*EE‿o* (io)
I am	*SO-no* (sono)

English	Pronunciation and Italian Spelling
I have	*O* (ho)
I don't have	*nohn O* (Non ho)
I want	*day-ZEE-day-ro* (desidero)
or	*VOHL-yo* (voglio)
ice cream	*jay-LA-to* (gelato)
in Italian	*een ee-tahl-YA-no* (in italiano)
ink	*eenk-YO-stro* (inchiostro)
iodine	*teen-TOO-ra DOHD-yo* (tintura d'odio)
is	*A Y* (è)
He is	*EL-yee A Y* (Egli è)
It is	*A Y* (è)
It is not	*nohn A Y* (Non è)
Is it far?	*A Y lohn-TA-no?* (È lontano?)
What is it?	*ko-ZA Y* (Cos'è?)
Where is it?	*do-VA Y?* (Dov'è?)
Where is there___?	*DO-vay CHA Y___?* (Dove c'è___?)
Italian	*ee-tahl-YA-no* (italiano)
in Italian	*een ee-tahl-YA-no* (in italiano)

K

kilometers	*kee-LO-may-tree* (chilometri)
knife	*kohl-TEL-lo* (coltello)

English	Pronunciation and Italian Spelling

L

lamb	*ahn-YEL-lo* (agnello)
laxative	*lahss-sa-TEE-vo* (lassativo)
leave	
it leaves	*PAR-tay* (parte)
left	
Turn left	*JEE-ra ah see-NEE-stra* (Gira a sinistra)
lemon	*lee-MO-nay* (limone)
lire	*LEE-ray* (lire)
lost	*spayr-DOO-to* (sperduto)
or	*spayr-DOO-tee* (sperduti)
luck	*for-TOO-na* (fortuna)
Good luck	*BWO-na for-TOO-na* (Buona fortuna)

M

madam	*seen-YO-ra* (signora)
main street	*STRA-da preen-chee-PA-lay* (strada principale)
map	*SKEET-tso* (schizzo)
Draw me a map	*FA-tay-mee oo-no SKEET-tso* (Fatemi uno schizzo)
market	*mayr-KA-to* (mercato)

Temple of Condord, Agrigento, Sicily

Duomo, Tuscany

English	Pronunciation and Italian Spelling
matches	*f˯yahm-MEE-fay-ree* (fiammiferi)
mattress	*ma-tay-RAHSS-so* (materasso)
me	*mee* (mi)
meat	*KAR-nay* (carne)
mechanic	*mek-KA-nee-ko* (meccanico)
milk	*LAHT-tay* (latte)
minus	*MAY-no* (meno)
minute	*mee-NOO-to* (minuto)
Wait a minute!	*ah-spet-TA-tay oon mee-NOO-to!* (Aspettate un minuto!)
miss	*seen-yo-REE-na* (signorina)
mister	*seen-YO-ray* (signore)
Monday	*loo-nay-DEE* (lunedì)
mosquito net	*dzahn-dzar-YAY-ra* (zanzariera)
movie	*FEELM* (film)
When does the movie start?	*ah KAY O-ra ko-MEEN-cha eel FEELM?* (A che ora comincia il film?)

N

name	
My name is___	*EE˯o mee K˯YA-mo___* (Io mi chiamo___)

47

English	Pronunciation and Italian Spelling
What is your name?	*KO-may see K‿YA-ma?* (Come si chiama?)
near	*vee-CHEE-no* (vicino)
the nearest town	*eel pa-AY-zay P‿YOO vee-CHEE-no* (il paese più vicino)
needle	*AH-go* (ago)
nine	*NO-vay* (nove)
nineteen	*dee-chahn-NO-vay* (diciannove)
ninety	*no-VAHN-ta* (novanta)
no	*NO* (no)
north	*NORD* (nord)
Which way is north?	*do-VAY eel NORD?* (Dov'e il nord?)
not	*NOHN* (non)

O

of	*dee* (di)
a bottle of wine	*oon F‿YA-sko dee VEE-no* (un fiasco di vino)
a cup of coffee	*oo-na TAHT-tsa dee kahf-FAY* (una tazza di caffè)
a cup of tea	*oo-na TAHT-tsa dee TAY* (una tazza di tè)
a glass of beer	*oon beek-K‿YAY-ray dee BEER-ra* (un bicchiere di birra)

English	Pronunciation and Italian Spelling
quarter of eight	*lay OHT-to MAY-no oon KWAR-to* (le otto meno un quarto)
or	*oon KWAR-to AHL-lay OHT-to* (un quarto alle otto)
one	*OO-no* (uno)
onions	*chee-POHL-lay* (cipolle)
orange	*ah-RAHN-cha* (arancia)

P

past

half past six	*lay SAY ay MED-dza* (le sei e mezza)
quarter past five	*lay CHEEN-kway ay oon KWAR-to* (le cinque e un quarto)
ten past two	*lay DOO-ay ay D⌣YAY-chee* (le due e dieci)

pay

I will pay you	*VEE pa-gay-RO* (Vi pagherò)
peas	*pee-ZEL-lee* (piselli)
pen	*PEN-na* (penna)
pencil	*ma-TEE-ta* (matita)
pepper	*PAY-pay* (pepe)
pillow	*koo-SHEE-no* (cuscino)

49

English	Pronunciation and Italian Spelling
pins	*SPEEL-lee* (spilli)
safety pins	*SPEEL-lee dee see-koo-RET-tsa* (spilli di sicurezza)
pipe	*PEE-pa* (pipa)
pipe tobacco	*ta-BAHK-ko payr PEE-pa* (tabacco per pipa)
plate	*P_YAHT-to* (piatto)
please	*payr fa-VO-ray* (per favore)
or	*payr p_ya-CHAY-ray* (per piacere)
point	
Point it out to me	*een-dee-KA-tay-mee* (Indicatemi)
police station	*kwess-TOO-ra* (questura)
policeman	*GWARD-ya* (guardia)
pork	*ma-YA-lay* (maiale)
porter	*fahk-KEE-no* (facchino)
post office	*oof-FEE-cho po-STA-lay* (ufficio postale)
potatoes	*pa-TA-tay* (patate)

Q

quarter	*KWAR-to* (quarto)
quarter of eight	*lay OHT-to MAY-no oon KWAR-to* (le otto meno un quarto)
or	*oon KWAR-to AHL-lay OHT-to* (un quarto alle otto)

English	Pronunciation and Italian Spelling
quarter past five	*lay CHEEN-kway ay oon KWAR-to* (le cinque e un quarto)
quickly	*PRESS-to* (presto)
Come quickly!	*vay-NEE-tay PRESS-to!* (Venite presto!)
Go quickly!	*ahn-DA-tay PRESS-to!* (Andate presto!)

R

railroad	*fayr-ro-VEE-ah* (ferrovia)
railroad station	*stahts-YO-nay* (stazione)
rain coat	*eem-payr-may-AH-bee-lay* (impermeabile)
razor	*ra-ZO-yo* (rasoio)
razor blades	*LA-may da ra-ZO-yo* (lame da rasoio)
rest	*ree-po-ZA-ray* (riposare)
restaurant	*ress-to-RAHN* (restaurant)
or	*ree-sto-RAHN-tay* (ristorante)
Where is the restaurant?	*do-VAY eel ress-to-RAHN?* (Dov'è il restaurant?)
rice	*REE-zo* (riso)

51

English	Pronunciation and Italian Spelling
right	
Turn right	*JEE-ra ah DESS-tra* (Gira a destra)
right away	*PRESS-to* (presto)
river	*F‿YOO-may* (fiume)
road	*STRA-da* (strada)
room	*KA-may-ra* (camera)

S

English	Pronunciation and Italian Spelling
safety pins	*SPEEL-lee dee see-koo-RET-tsa* (spilli di sicurezza)
salad	*een-sa-LA-ta* (insalata)
salt	*SA-lay* (sale)
Saturday	*SA-ba-to* (sabato)
say	
How do you say___?	*KO-may see K‿YA-ma___?* (Come si chiama___?)
or	*KO-may see DEE-chay___?* (Come si dice___?)
servant	*oon ka-mayr-YAY-ray* (un cameriere)
seven	*SET-tay* (sette)
seventeen	*dee-chass-SET-tay* (diciassette)
seventy	*set-TAHN-ta* (settanta)

English	Pronunciation and Italian Spelling
shave	
I want to be shaved	*day-ZEE-day-ro FAR-mee la BAR-ba* (Desidero farmi la barba)
shaving brush	*pen-NEL-lo payr BAR-ba* (pennello payr barba)
shaving soap	*sa-PO-nay payr BAR-ba* (sapone per barba)
she	*ESS-sa* (essa)
sheets	*lent-SWO-la* (lenzuola)
shirt	*ka-MEE-cha* (camicia)
shoes	*SKAR-pay* (scarpe)
shoe laces	*LAHT-chee da SKAR-pay* (lacci da scarpe)
shoe polish	*CHAY-ra payr SKAR-pay* (cera per scarpe)
shoemaker	*kahl-tso-LA-yo* (calzolaio)
sick	*ahm-ma-LA-to* (ammalato)
or	*ahm-ma-LA-tee* (ammalati)
sir	*seen-YO-ray* (signore)
six	*SAY* (sei)
sixteen	*SAY-dee-chee* (sedici)
sixty	*sess-SAHN-ta* (sessanta)
sleep	*dor-MEE-ray* (dormire)
slowly	*ah-DA-jo* (adagio)
soap	*sa-PO-nay* (sapone)

English	Pronunciation and Italian Spelling
soldiers	*sohl-DA-tee* (soldati)
soup	*mee-NESS-tra* (minestra)
speak	*par-LA-tay* (parlate)
Speak slowly	*par-LA-tay ah-DA-jo* (Parlate adagio)
spinach	*spee-NA-chee* (spinaci)
spoon	*kook-K⁀YA-yo* (cucchiaio)
spring	*sor-JEN-tay* (sorgente)
start	
it starts	*ko-MEEN-cha* (comincia)
When does the movie start?	*ah KAY O-ra ko-MEEN-cha eel FEELM?* (A che ora comincia il film?)
station	*stahts-YO-nay* (stazione)
Where is the railroad station?	*do-VAY la stahts-YO-nay?* (Dov'è la stazione?)
steak	*bee-STEK-ka* (bistecca)
Stop!	*fayr-MA-tay-vee!* (Fermatevi!)
straight ahead	*dee-REET-to* (diritto)
street	*STRA-da* (strada)
main street	*STRA-da preen-chee-PA-lay* (strada principale)
sugar	*TSOOK-kay-ro* (zucchero)
Sunday	*do-MAY-nee-ka* (domenica)

54

Florence

Square, Radda

T

tailor	*SAR-to* (sarto)
take	
take a bath	*PREN-day-ray oon BAHN-yo* (prendere un bagno)
Take cover!	*MET-tayr-see ahl ree-PA-ro!* (Mettersi al riparo!)
Take me there	*ahk-kohm-pahn-YA-tay-mee LA* (Accompagnatemi là)
Take me to a doctor	*ahk-kohm-pahn-YA-tay-mee da oon MAY-dee-ko* (Accompagnatemi da un medico)
Take me to the hospital	*ahk-kohm-pahn-YA-tay-mee ahl-lo-spay-DA-lay* (Accompagnatemi all'ospedale)
tea	*TAY* (tè)
a cup of tea	*oo-na TAHT-tsa dee TAY* (una tazza di tè)
telegraph office	*loof-FEE-cho tay-lay-GRA-fee-ko* (l'ufficio telegrafico)
telephone	*tay-LAY-fo-no* (telefono)
ten	*D͜YAY-chee* (dieci)
thank you	*GRAHTS-yay* (grazie)
the	*eel* (il)
or	*la* (la)
or	*ee* (i)

English	Pronunciation and Italian Spelling
there	*LA* (là)
Take me there	*ahk-kohm-pahn-YA-tay-mee LA* (Accompagnatemi là)
they	*ESS-see* (essi)
thirsty	
I am thirsty	*O SAY-tay* (Ho sete)
thirteen	*TRAY-dee-chee* (tredici)
thirty	*TREN-ta* (trenta)
thirty-one	*tren-TOO-no* (trentuno)
thirty-two	*tren-ta-DOO-ay* (trentadue)
this	*KWESS-to* (questo)
What's this?	*ko-ZAY KWESS-to?* (Cos'è questo?)
thousand	*MEEL-lay* (mille)
thread	*FEE-lo* (filo)
three	*TRAY* (tre)
Thursday	*jo-vay-DEE* (giovedì)
time	
At what time?	*ah KAY O-ra?* (A che ora?)
What time is it?	*kay O-ra AY?* (Che ora è?)

English		Pronunciation and Italian Spelling
tired		*STAHN-ko* (stanco)
	or	*STAHN-kee* (stanchi)
to		
to a doctor		*da oon MAY-dee-ko* (da un medico)
to a hospital		*ahl-lo-spay-DA-lay* (all'ospedale)
three minutes to nine		*lay NO-vay MAY-no TRAY* (le nove meno tre)
tobacco		*ta-BAHK-ko* (tabacco)
pipe tobacco		*ta-BAHK-ko payr PEE-pa* (tabacco per pipa)
today		*OHD-jee* (oggi)
toilet		*ga-bee-NET-to* (gabinetto)
Where is a toilet?		*do-VAY eel ga-bee-NET-to?* (Dov'è il gabinetto?)
tomato		*po-mo-DO-ro* (pomodoro)
tomorrow		*do-MA-nee* (domani)
too expensive		*TROHP-po KA-ro* (troppo caro)
tooth paste		*PA-sta den-tee-FREE-cha* (pasta dentifricia)
toothbrush		*spaht-tso-LEE-no da DEN-tee* (spazzolino di denti)
towel		*ah-shoo-ga-MA-no* (asciugamano)
town		*pa-AY-zay* (paese)

English	Pronunciation and Italian Spelling
the nearest town	*eel pa-AY-zay P‿YOO vee-CHEE-no* (il paese più vicino)
train	*TRAY-no* (treno)
When does the train leave?	*ah KAY O-ra PAR-tay eel TRAY-no?* (A che ora parte il treno?)
Tuesday	*mar-tay-DEE* (martedì)
Turn!	*JEE-ra!* (Gira!)
Turn left	*JEE-ra ah see-NEE-stra* (Gira a sinistra)
Turn right	*JEE-ra ah DESS-tra* (Gira a destra)
twelve	*DO-dee-chee* (dodici)
twenty	*VEN-tee* (venti)
twenty-one	*ven-TOO-no* (ventuno)
twenty-two	*ven-tee-DOO-ay* (ventidue)
two	*DOO-ay* (due)
two o'clock	*SO-no lay DOO-ay* (Sono le due)

U

English	Pronunciation and Italian Spelling
undershirt	*MAHL-ya* (maglia)
undershorts	*moo-TAHN-day* (mutande)
understand	
Do you understand?	*ah-VAY-tay ka-PEE-to?* (Avete capito?)
I don't understand	*NOHN ka-PEE-sko* (Non capisco)

English	Pronunciation and Italian Spelling

V

veal	*vee-TEL-lo* (vitello)
vegetables	*vayr-DOO-ra* (verdura)
or	*lay-GOO-mee* (legumi)

W

Wait a minute!	*ah-spet-TA-tay oon mee-NOO-to!*
	(Aspettate un minuto!)

want

I want___ *or* I want to___	*day-ZEE-day-ro___* (desidero___)
or	*VOHL-yo___* (voglio___)
We want___	*day-zee-dayr-YA-mo* (desideriamo)

wash up

I want to wash up	*day-ZEE-day-ro la-VAR-mee* (Desidero lavarmi)
Watch out!	*aht-tents-YO-nay!* (Attenzione!)
water	*AHK-kwa* (acqua)
boiled water	*AHK-kwa bohl-LEE-ta* (acqua bollita)
drinking water	*AHK-kwa po-TA-bee-lay* (acqua potabile)
hot water	*AHK-kwa KAHL-da* (acqua calda)

59

English	Pronunciation and Italian Spelling
we	
We are	S‿YA-mo (Siamo)
We have	abh-B‿YA-mo (Abbiamo)
We don't have	nohn ahb-B‿YA-mo (Non abbiamo)
We want___	day-zee-dayr-YA-mo___ (Desideriamo___)
Wednesday	mayr-ko-lay-DEE (mercoledì)
well (for water)	POHT-tso (pozzo)
well	BAY-nay (bene)
I am well	STO BAY-nay (Sto bene)
what	KO-za (cosa)
At what time	ah KAY O-ra (A che ora?)
What is this?	ko-ZAY KWESS-to? (Cos'è questo?)
What is your name?	KO-may see K‿YA-ma? (Come si chiama?)
What time is it?	kay O-ra AY? (Che ora è?)
when	
When does the movie start?	ah KAY O-ra ko-MEEN-cha eel FEELM? (A che ora comincia il film?)
When does the train leave?	ah KAY O-ra PAR-tay eel TRAY-no? (A che ora parte il treno?)

English	Pronunciation and Italian Spelling
where	*DO-vay* (dove)
Where are they?	*DO-vay SO-no?* (Dove sono?)
Where is it?	*do-VAY?* (Dov'è?)
Where is there___?	*DO-vay CHAY___?* (Dove c'è___?)
Where can I find *or* get___?	*DO-vay POHSS-so tro-VA-ray___?* (Dove posso trovare___?)
which	*KWA-lay* (quale)
Which is the road to___?	*kwa-LAY la STRA-da payr___?* (Qual'è la strada per___?)
Which way is north?	*do-VAY eel NORD?* (Dov'è il nord?)
wine	*VEE-no* (vino)
a bottle of wine	*oon F⁀YA-sko dee VEE-no* (un fiasco di vino)
workman	*o-pay-RA-yo* (operaio)
wounded	*fay-REE-to* (ferito)
or	*fay-REE-tee* (feriti)

Y

yes	*SEE* (sì)
yesterday	*YAY-ree* (ieri)
you	*VOY* (voi)
Are you?	*S⁀YAY-tay?* (Siete?)
Have you?	*ah-VAY-tay?* (Avete?)
I will pay you	*vee pa-gay-RO* (Vi pagherò)

Il Battistero with Duomo, Pisa

62